let's cook

italian

GW00685483

Penny
Stephens

p

Contents

Tuscan Bean Soup

A thick and creamy soup that is based on a traditional Tuscan recipe.
It is delicious served with fresh, warm bread and butter.

Serves 4

INGREDIENTS

225 g/8 oz dried butter beans soaked
   overnight or 2 x 420 g/14^1/$_2$ oz can
   butter beans
1 tbsp olive oil

2 garlic cloves, crushed
1 vegetable or chicken stock cube,
   crumbled
150 ml/5 fl oz/^{2}/$_3$ cup milk

2 tbsp chopped fresh oregano
salt and pepper

1 If you are using dried beans that have been soaked overnight, drain them thoroughly. Bring a large pan of water to the boil, add the beans and boil for 10 minutes. Cover the pan and simmer for a further 30 minutes or until tender. Drain the beans, reserving the cooking liquid. If you are using canned beans, drain them thoroughly and reserve the liquid.

2 Heat the oil in a large frying pan (skillet) and fry the garlic for 2–3 minutes or until just beginning to brown.

3 Add the beans and 400 ml/ 14 fl oz/1^2/$_3$ cup of the reserved liquid to the pan (skillet), stirring. You may need to add a little water if there is insufficient liquid. Stir in the crumbled stock cube. Bring the mixture to the boil and then remove the pan from the heat.

4 Place the bean mixture in a food processor and blend to form a smooth purée. Alternatively, mash the bean mixture to a smooth consistency. Season to taste with salt and pepper and stir in the milk.

5 Pour the soup back into the pan and gently heat to just below boiling point. Stir in the chopped oregano just before serving.

VARIATION

If you prefer, use 3 teaspoons of dried oregano instead of fresh, but add with the beans in step 3. This soup can also be made with cannelini or borlotti beans following the same method.

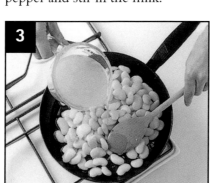

Minestrone

*Minestrone translates as 'big soup' in Italian. It is made all over Italy,
but this version comes from Livorno, a port on the western coast.*

Serves 4

INGREDIENTS

1 tbsp olive oil
100 g/3¹/₂ oz pancetta ham, diced
2 medium onions, chopped
2 cloves garlic, crushed
1 potato, peeled and cut into
    10 mm/¹/₂ inch cubes
1 carrot, scraped and cut into chunks
1 leek, sliced into rings

¹/₄ green cabbage, shredded
1 stick celery, chopped
1 x 450 g/1 lb can chopped tomatoes
1 x 210 g/7 oz can flageolet `(small
    navy) beans, drained and rinsed
600 ml/1 pint/2¹/₂ cups hot ham or
    chicken stock diluted with 600 ml/
    1 pint/2¹/₂ cups boiling water

bouquet garni (2 bay leaves, 2 sprigs
    rosemary and 2 sprigs thyme, tied
    together)
salt and pepper
freshly grated Parmesan cheese,
    to serve

1 Heat the oil in a large
saucepan. Add the diced
pancetta, chopped onions and
garlic and fry for about 5 minutes
or until the onions are soft and
golden.

2 Add the prepared potato,
carrot, leek, cabbage and
celery to the saucepan. Cook
for a further 2 minutes, stirring
frequently, to coat all of the
vegetables in the oil.

3 Add the tomatoes, flageolet
(small navy) beans, hot ham
or chicken stock and bouquet
garni to the pan, stirring to
mix. Leave the soup to simmer,
covered, for 15–20 minutes or
until all of the vegetables are
just tender.

4 Remove the bouquet garni,
season with salt and pepper
to taste and serve with plenty of
freshly grated Parmesan.

VARIATION

*Any combination of vegetables
will work equally well in this soup.
For a special minestrone, try adding
100 g/3¹/₂ oz Parma ham
(prosciutto), shredded, in step 1.*

Fresh Figs with Parma Ham (Prosciutto)

This colourful fresh salad is delicious at any time of the year.

Serves 4

INGREDIENTS

40 g/1¹/₂ oz rocket (arugula)
4 fresh figs
4 slices Parma ham (prosciutto)

4 tbsp olive oil
1 tbsp fresh orange juice

1 tbsp clear honey
1 small red chilli

1 Tear the rocket (arugula) into more manageable pieces and arrange on 4 serving plates.

2 Using a sharp knife, cut each of the figs into quarters and place them on top of the rocket (arugula) leaves.

3 Using a sharp knife, cut the Parma ham (prosciutto) into strips and scatter over the rocket (arugula) and figs.

4 Place the oil, orange juice and honey in a screw-top jar. Shake the jar until the mixture emulsifies and forms a thick dressing. Transfer to a bowl.

5 Using a sharp knife, dice the chilli, remembering not to touch your face before you have washed your hands (see Cook's Tip, right). Add the chopped chilli to the dressing and mix well.

6 Drizzle the dressing over the Parma ham (prosciutto), rocket (arugula) and figs, tossing to mix well. Serve at once.

COOK'S TIP

Parma, in the Emilia-Romagna region of Italy, is famous for its ham, prosciutto di Parma, thought to be the best in the world.

COOK'S TIP

Chillies can burn the skin for several hours after chopping, so it is advisable to wear gloves when you are handling the very hot varieties .

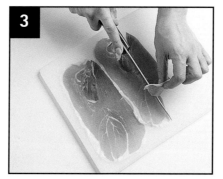

Tuscan Bean Salad with Tuna

The combination of beans and tuna is a favourite with the people of Tuscany. The hint of honey and lemon in the dressing makes this salad refreshing as well as hearty.

Serves 4

INGREDIENTS

1 small white onion or 2 spring onions (scallions), finely chopped
2 x 400g/14 oz cans butter beans, drained

2 medium tomatoes
1 x 185 g/6^1/$_2$ oz can tuna, drained
2 tbsp flat leaf parsley, chopped
2 tbsp olive oil

1 tbsp lemon juice
2 tsp clear honey
1 garlic clove, crushed

1 Place the chopped onions or spring onions (scallions) and butter beans in a bowl and mix well to combine.

2 Using a sharp knife, cut the tomatoes into wedges. Add the tomatoes to the onion and bean mixture.

3 Flake the tuna with a fork and add it to the onion and bean mixture together with the parsley.

4 In a screw-top jar, mix together the olive oil, lemon juice, honey and garlic. Shake the jar until the dressing emulsifies and thickens.

5 Pour the dressing over the bean salad. Toss the ingredients together using 2 spoons and serve.

COOK'S TIP

This salad will keep for several days in a covered container in the refrigerator. Make up the dressing just before serving and toss the ingredients together to mix well.

VARIATION

Substitute fresh salmon for the tuna if you wish to create a luxurious version of this recipe for a special occasion.

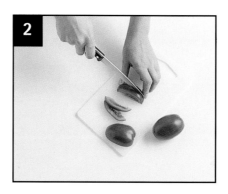

Capri Salad

*This tomato, olive and Mozzarella salad, dressed with balsamic vinegar and olive oil, makes
a delicious starter on its own. Increase the quantity by half to make for a full salad for four people.*

Serves 4

INGREDIENTS

2 beef tomatoes
125 g/4^1/2 oz Mozzarella cheese
12 black olives

8 basil leaves
1 tbsp balsamic vinegar
1 tbsp olive oil

salt and pepper
basil leaves, to garnish

1 Using a sharp knife, cut the tomatoes into thin slices.

2 Using a sharp knife, cut the Mozzarella into slices.

3 Pit the olives and slice them into rings.

4 Layer the tomato, Mozzarella cheese and olives in a stack, finishing with a layer of cheese on top.

5 Place each stack under a preheated hot grill (broiler) for 2–3 minutes or just long enough to melt the Mozzarella.

6 Drizzle over the vinegar and olive oil, and season to taste with salt and pepper.

7 Transfer to serving plates and garnish with basil leaves. Serve immediately.

COOK'S TIP

Buffalo mozzarella cheese, although it is usually more expensive because of the comparative rarity of buffalo, does have a better flavour than the cow's milk variety. It is popular in salads, but also provides a tangy layer in baked dishes.

COOK'S TIP

Balsamic vinegar, which has grown in popularity over the past decade, is produced in the Emilia-Romagna region of Italy. It is made from wine which is distilled until it is dark brown and extremely strongly flavoured.

Bruschetta with Tomatoes

*Using ripe tomatoes and the best olive oil will
make this Tuscan dish absolutely delicious.*

Serves 4

INGREDIENTS

300 g/10^{1}/$_{2}$ oz cherry tomatoes

4 sun-dried tomatoes

4 tbsp extra virgin olive oil

16 fresh basil leaves, shredded

8 slices ciabatta

2 garlic cloves, peeled

salt and pepper

1 Using a sharp knife, cut the cherry tomatoes in half.

2 Using a sharp knife, slice the sun-dried tomatoes into strips.

3 Place the cherry tomatoes and sun-dried tomatoes in a bowl. Add the olive oil and the shredded basil leaves and toss to mix well. Season to taste with a little salt and pepper.

4 Using a sharp knife, cut the garlic cloves in half. Lightly toast the ciabatta bread.

5 Rub the garlic, cut-side down, over both sides of the toasted ciabatta bread.

6 Top the ciabatta bread with the tomato mixture and serve immediately.

COOK'S TIP

*Ciabatta is an Italian rustic
bread which is slightly holey
and quite chewy. It is very good
in this recipe as it absorbs the
full flavour of the garlic and
extra virgin olive oil.*

VARIATION

*Plum tomatoes are also good in this
recipe. Halve them, then cut them
into wedges. Mix them with the
sun-dried tomatoes in step 3.*

Potatoes with Olives & Anchovies

This side dish makes a delicious accompaniment for grilled fish or for lamb chops.
The fennel adds a subtle aniseed flavour.

Serves 4

INGREDIENTS

450 g/1lb baby new potatoes, scrubbed

2 tbsp olive oil

2 fennel bulbs, trimmed and sliced

2 sprigs rosemary, stalks removed

75 g/2^3/4 oz mixed olives

8 canned anchovy fillets, drained and chopped

1 Bring a large saucepan of water to the boil and cook the potatoes for 8–10 minutes or until tender. Remove the potatoes from the saucepan using a perforated spoon and set aside to cool slightly.

2 Once the potatoes are just cool enough to handle, cut them into wedges, using a sharp knife.

3 Pit the mixed olives and cut them in half, using a sharp knife.

4 Using a sharp knife, chop the anchovy fillets into smaller strips.

5 Heat the oil in a large frying pan (skillet). Add the potato wedges, sliced fennel and rosemary. Cook for 7–8 minutes or until the potatoes are golden.

6 Stir in the olives and anchovies and cook for 1 minute or until warmed through.

7 Transfer to serving plates and serve immediately.

COOK'S TIP

Fresh rosemary is a particular favourite with Italians, but you can experiment with your favourite herbs in this recipe, if you prefer.

Onion & Mozzarella Tarts

These individual tarts are delicious hot or cold and are great for picnics.

Serves 4

INGREDIENTS

1 x 250g/9 oz packet puff pastry, defrosted if frozen

2 medium red onions, cut into thin wedges

1 red (bell) pepper, halved and deseeded

8 cherry tomatoes, halved

100g/3 $^3/_4$ oz Mozzarella cheese, cut into chunks

8 sprigs thyme

---

1 Roll out the pastry to make 4 x 7.5 cm/3 inch squares. Using a sharp knife, trim the edges of the pastry, reserving the trimmings. Leave the pastry to chill in the refrigerator for 30 minutes.

2 Place the pastry squares on a baking tray (cookie sheet). Brush a little water along each edge of the pastry squares and use the reserved pastry trimmings to make a rim around each tart.

3 Cut the red onions into wedges and halve and deseed the (bell) peppers.

4 Place the onions and (bell) pepper in a roasting tin (pan). Cook under a preheated grill (broiler) for 15 minutes or until charred.

5 Place the roasted (bell) pepper halves in a polythene bag and leave to sweat for 10 minutes. Peel off the skin from the (bell) peppers and cut the flesh into strips.

6 Line the pastry squares with squares of foil. Bake in a preheated oven at 200°C/400°F/ Gas Mark 6 for 10 minutes. Remove the foil squares and bake for a further 5 minutes.

7 Place the onions, (bell) pepper strips, tomatoes and cheese in each tart and sprinkle with the fresh thyme.

8 Return to the oven for 15 minutes or until the pastry is golden. Serve hot.

Sardinian Red Mullet

*Red mullet has a beautiful pink skin, which is enhanced in this dish
by being cooked in red wine and orange juice.*

Serves 4

INGREDIENTS

50 g/1³/₄ oz sultanas
150 ml/5 fl oz/²/₃ cup red wine
2 tbsp olive oil
2 medium onions, sliced

1 courgette (zucchini), cut into
  5 cm/2 inch sticks
2 oranges
2 tsp coriander seeds, lightly crushed

4 red mullet, boned and filleted
1 x 50g/1³/₄ oz can anchovy fillets,
  drained
2 tbsp chopped, fresh oregano

1 Place the sultanas in a bowl. Pour over the red wine and leave to soak for 10 minutes.

2 Heat the oil in a large frying pan (skillet). Add the onions and sauté for 2 minutes.

3 Add the courgettes (zucchini) to the pan and fry for a further 3 minutes or until tender.

4 Using a zester, pare long, thin strips from one of the oranges. Using a sharp knife, remove the skin from both of the oranges, then segment the oranges by slicing between the lines of pith.

5 Add the orange zest to the frying pan (skillet). Add the red wine, sultanas, red mullet and anchovies to the pan and leave to simmer for 10–15 minutes or until the fish is cooked through.

6 Stir in the oregano, set aside and leave to cool. Place the mixture in a large bowl and leave to chill, covered, in the refrigerator for at least 2 hours to allow the flavours to mingle. Transfer to serving plates and serve.

COOK'S TIP

Red mullet is usually available all year round – frozen, if not fresh – from your fishmonger or supermarket. If you cannot get hold of it try using telapia. This dish can also be served warm, if you prefer.

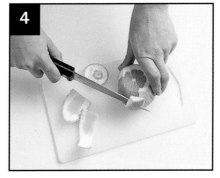

Fresh Baked Sardines

Here, fresh sardines are baked with eggs, herbs and vegetables to form a dish similar to an omelette.

Serves 4

INGREDIENTS

2 tbsp olive oil
2 large onions, sliced into rings
3 garlic cloves, chopped
2 large courgettes (zucchini), cut into
  sticks

3 tbsp fresh thyme, stalks removed
8 sardine fillets or about 1 kg/
  2 lb 4 oz whole sardines, filleted
75 g/2³/₄ oz Parmesan cheese, grated

4 eggs, beaten
150 ml/5 fl oz/²/₃ pint milk
salt and pepper

---

1 Heat 1 tablespoon of the oil in a frying pan (skillet). Add the onions and garlic and sauté for 2–3 minutes.

2 Add the courgettes (zucchini) to the frying pan (skillet) and cook for about 5 minutes or until golden.

3 Stir 2 tablespoons of the thyme into the mixture.

4 Place half of the onions and courgettes (zucchini) in the base of a large ovenproof dish. Top with the sardine fillets and half of the Parmesan cheese.

5 Place the remaining onions and courgettes (zucchini) on top and sprinkle with the remaining thyme.

6 Mix the eggs and milk together in a bowl and season to taste with salt and pepper. Pour the mixture over the vegetables and sardines in the dish. Sprinkle the remaining Parmesan cheese over the top.

7 Bake in a preheated oven at 180°C/350°F/Gas Mark 4 for 20–25 minutes or until golden and set. Serve hot, straight from the oven.

VARIATION

If you cannot find sardines that are large enough to fillet, use small mackerel instead.

Italian Cod

Cod roasted with herbs and topped with a lemon and rosemary crust is a delicious main course.

Serves 4

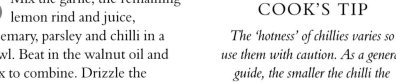

INGREDIENTS

25 g/1 oz/2 tbsp butter
50 g/1³/₄ oz wholemeal breadcrumbs
25 g/1 oz chopped walnuts
grated rind and juice of 2 lemons

2 sprigs rosemary, stalks removed
2 tbsp chopped parsley
4 cod fillets, each about 150 g/
  5¹/₂ oz

1 garlic clove, crushed
3 tbsp walnut oil
1 small red chilli, diced
salad leaves, to serve

1 Melt the butter in a large frying pan (skillet).

2 Remove the frying pan (skillet) from the heat and add the breadcrumbs, walnuts, the rind and juice of 1 lemon, half of the rosemary and half of the parsley.

3 Press the breadcrumb mixture over the top of the cod fillets. Place the cod fillets in a shallow, foil-lined roasting tin (pan).

4 Bake in a preheated oven at 200°C/400°F/Gas Mark 6 for 25–30 minutes.

5 Mix the garlic, the remaining lemon rind and juice, rosemary, parsley and chilli in a bowl. Beat in the walnut oil and mix to combine. Drizzle the dressing over the cod steaks as soon as they are cooked.

6 Transfer to serving plates and serve immediately.

VARIATION

If preferred, the walnuts may be omitted from the crust. In addition, extra virgin olive oil can be used instead of walnut oil, if you prefer.

COOK'S TIP

The 'hotness' of chillies varies so use them with caution. As a general guide, the smaller the chilli the hotter it will be.

Rich Beef Stew

This slow-cooked beef stew is flavoured with oranges, red wine and porcini mushrooms.

Serves 4

INGREDIENTS

1 tbsp oil
15 g/$^1/_2$ oz/1 tbsp butter
225 g/8 oz baby onions, peeled and
   halved

600 g/1 lb 5 oz stewing steak, diced
   into 4 cm/1$^1/_2$ inch chunks
300 ml/$^1/_2$ pint/1$^1/_4$ cup beef stock
150 ml/5 fl oz/$^2/_3$ cup red wine
4 tbsp chopped oregano
1 tbsp sugar

1 orange
25 g/1 oz porcini or other dried
   mushrooms
225 g/8 oz fresh plum tomatoes
cooked rice or potatoes, to serve

1 Heat the oil and butter in a large frying pan (skillet). Add the onions and sauté for 5 minutes or until golden. Remove with a perforated spoon, set aside and keep warm.

2 Add the beef to the pan and cook, stirring, for 5 minutes or until browned all over.

3 Return the onions to the frying pan (skillet) and add the stock, wine, oregano and sugar, stirring to mix well. Transfer the mixture to an ovenproof casserole dish.

4 Pare the rind from the orange and cut it into strips. Slice the orange flesh into rings. Add the orange rings and the rind to the casserole. Cook in a preheated oven, at 180°C/350°F/Gas Mark 4, for 1$^1/_4$ hours.

5 Soak the porcini mushrooms for 30 minutes in a small bowl containing 4 tablespoons of warm water.

6 Peel and halve the tomatoes. Add the tomatoes, porcini mushrooms and their soaking liquid to the casserole. Cook for a further 20 minutes until the beef is tender and the juices thickened. Serve with cooked rice or potatoes.

VARIATION

Instead of fresh tomatoes, try using 8 sun-dried tomatoes, cut into wide strips, if you prefer.

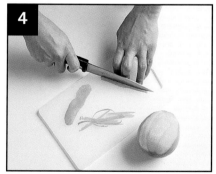

Neapolitan Pork Steaks

An Italian version of grilled pork steaks, this dish is easy to make and delicious to eat.

Serves 4

INGREDIENTS

2 tbsp olive oil
1 garlic clove, chopped
1 large onion, sliced
1 x 400 g/14 oz can tomatoes

2 tsp yeast extract
4 pork loin steaks, each about
  125 g/4^1/$_2$ oz
75 g/2^3/$_4$ oz black olives, pitted

2 tbsp fresh basil, shredded
freshly grated Parmesan cheese, to
  serve

1 Heat the oil in a large frying pan (skillet). Add the onions and garlic and cook, stirring, for 3–4 minutes or until they just begin to soften.

2 Add the tomatoes and yeast extract to the frying pan (skillet) and leave to simmer for about 5 minutes or until the sauce starts to thicken.

3 Cook the pork steaks, under a preheated grill (broiler), for 5 minutes on both sides, until the the meat is golden and cooked through. Set the pork steaks aside and keep warm.

4 Add the olives and fresh shredded basil to the sauce in the frying pan (skillet) and stir quickly to combine.

5 Transfer the steaks to warm serving plates. Top the steaks with the sauce, sprinkle with freshly grated Parmesan cheese and serve immediately.

COOK'S TIP

Parmesan is a mature and exceptionally hard cheese produced in Italy. You only need to add a little as it has a very strong flavour.

COOK'S TIP

There are many types of canned tomato available – for example plum tomatoes, or tomatoes chopped in water, or chopped sieved tomatoes (passata). The chopped variety are often canned with added flavours such as garlic, basil, onion, chilli and mixed herbs, and are a good storecupboard standby.

Roman Pan-fried Lamb

Chunks of tender lamb, pan-fried with garlic and stewed in red wine are a real Roman dish.

Serves 4

INGREDIENTS

1 tbsp oil
15 g/$^1/_2$ oz/1 tbsp butter
600 g/1 lb 5 oz lamb (shoulder or
   leg), cut in 2.5 cm/1 inch chunks
4 garlic cloves, peeled

3 sprigs thyme, stalks removed
6 canned anchovy fillets
150 ml/5 fl oz/$^2/_3$ cup red wine
150 ml/5 fl oz/$^2/_3$ cup lamb or
   vegetable stock

1 tsp sugar
50 g/1$^3/_4$ oz black olives, pitted and
   halved
2 tbsp chopped parsley, to garnish
mashed potato, to serve

1 Heat the oil and butter in a large frying pan (skillet). Add the lamb and cook for 4–5 minutes, stirring, until the meat is browned all over.

2 Using a pestle and mortar, grind together the garlic, thyme and anchovies to make a smooth paste.

3 Add the wine and lamb or vegetable stock to the frying pan (skillet). Stir in the garlic and anchovy paste together with the sugar.

4 Bring the mixture to the boil, reduce the heat, cover and leave to simmer for 30–40 minutes or until the lamb is tender. For the last 10 minutes of the cooking time, remove the lid in order to allow the sauce to reduce slightly.

5 Stir the olives into the sauce and mix to combine.

6 Transfer the lamb and the sauce to a serving bowl and garnish with freshly chopped parsley. Serve with creamy mashed potatoes.

COOK'S TIP

Rome is the capital of both the region of Lazio and Italy and thus has become a focal point for specialities from all over Italy. Food from this region tends to be fairly simple and quick to prepare, all with plenty of herbs and seasonings giving really robust flavours.

Chicken Marengo

Napoleon's chef was ordered to cook a sumptuous meal on the eve of the battle of Marengo.
He gathered everything possible to make a feast, and this was the result.

Serves 4

INGREDIENTS

1 tbsp olive oil
8 chicken pieces
300 g/10^1/$_2$ oz passata (tomato
   paste)
200 ml/7 fl oz/^{3}/$_4$ cup white wine
2 tsp dried mixed herbs

8 slices white bread
40 g/1^1/$_2$ oz butter, melted
2 garlic cloves, crushed
100 g/3^1/$_2$ oz mixed mushrooms
   (such as button, oyster and ceps)

40 g/1^3/$_4$ oz black olives, chopped
1 tsp sugar
fresh basil, to garnish

1 Using a sharp knife, remove the bone from each of the chicken pieces.

2 Heat the oil in a large frying pan (skillet). Add the chicken pieces and cook for 4–5 minutes, turning occassionally, or until browned all over.

3 Add the passata (tomato paste), wine and mixed herbs to the frying pan (skillet). Bring to the boil and then leave to simmer for 30 minutes or until the chicken is tender and the juices run clear when a skewer is inserted into the thickest part of the meat.

4 Mix the melted butter and crushed garlic together. Lightly toast the slices of bread and brush with the garlic butter.

5 Add the remaining oil to a separate frying pan (skillet) and cook the mushrooms for 2–3 minutes or until just brown.

6 Add the olives and sugar to the chicken mixture and warm through.

7 Transfer the chicken and sauce to serving plates. Serve with the bruschetta (fried bread) and fried mushrooms.

COOK'S TIP

If you have time, marinate the chicken pieces in the wine and herbs and leave in the refrigerator for 2 hours. This will make the chicken more tender and accentuate the wine flavour of the sauce.

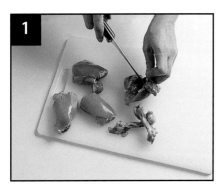

Parma-wrapped Chicken

There is a delicious surprise inside these chicken breast parcels!

Serves 4

INGREDIENTS

4 chicken breasts, skin removed
100 g/3¹/₂ oz full fat soft cheese,
    flavoured with herbs and garlic

8 slices Parma ham (prosciutto)
150 ml/5 fl oz/²/₃ cup red wine

150 ml/5 fl oz/²/₃ cup chicken stock
1 tbsp brown sugar

1 Using a sharp knife, make a horizontal slit along the length of each chicken breast to form a pocket.

2 Beat the cheese with a wooden spoon to soften it. Spoon the cheese into the pocket of the chicken breasts.

3 Wrap 2 slices of Parma ham (prosciutto) around each chicken breast and secure in place with a length of string.

4 Pour the wine and chicken stock into a large frying pan (skillet) and bring to the boil. When the mixture is just starting to boil, add the sugar and stir to dissolve.

5 Add the chicken breasts to the mixture in the frying pan (skillet). Leave to simmer for 12–15 minutes or the chicken is tender and the juices run clear when a skewer is inserted into the thickest part of the meat.

6 Remove the chicken from the pan, set aside and keep warm.

7 Reheat the sauce and boil until reduced and thickened. Remove the string from the chicken and cut into slices. Pour the sauce over the chicken to serve.

VARIATION

Try adding 2 finely chopped sun-dried tomatoes to the soft cheese in step 2, if you prefer.

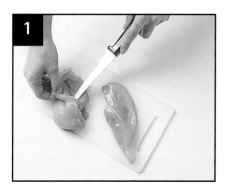

Basil & Tomato Pasta

Roasting the tomatoes gives a sweeter and smoother flavour to this sauce. Try to buy Italian tomatoes, such as plum or flavia, as these have a better flavour and colour.

Serves 4

INGREDIENTS

1 tbsp olive oil
2 sprigs rosemary
2 cloves garlic, unpeeled

450 g/1 lb tomatoes, halved
1 tbsp sun-dried tomato paste
12 fresh basil leaves, plus extra to garnish

salt and pepper
675 g/1^1/$_2$ lb fresh farfalle or 350 g/12 oz dried farfalle

1 Place the oil, rosemary, garlic and tomatoes, skin side up, in a shallow roasting tin (pan).

2 Drizzle with a little oil and cook under a preheated grill (broiler) for 20 minutes or until the tomato skins are slightly charred.

3 Peel the skin from the tomatoes. Roughly chop the tomato flesh and place in a pan.

4 Squeeze the pulp from the garlic cloves and mix with the tomato flesh and sun-dried tomato paste.

5 Roughly tear the fresh basil leaves into smaller pieces and then stir them into the sauce. Season with a little salt and pepper to taste.

6 Cook the farfalle in a saucepan of boiling water according to the instructions on the packet or until it is cooked through, but still has 'bite'. Drain.

7 Gently heat the tomato and basil sauce.

8 Transfer the farfalle to serving plates and serve with the basil and tomato sauce.

COOK'S TIP

This sauce tastes just as good when served cold in a pasta salad.

Pasta & Sicilian Sauce

*This Sicilian recipe of anchovies mixed with pine nuts
and sultanas in a tomato sauce is delicious with all types of pasta.*

Serves 4

INGREDIENTS

450 g/1lb tomatoes, halved
25 g/1 oz pine nuts
50 g/1³/₄ oz sultanas

1 x 50 g/1³/₄ oz can anchovies,
  drained and halved lengthways
2 tbsp concentrated tomato purée

675 g/1¹/₂ lb fresh or 350 g/12 oz
  dried penne

1 Cook the tomatoes under a preheated grill (broiler) for about 10 minutes. Leave to cool slightly, then once cool enough to handle, peel off the skin and dice the flesh.

2 Place the pine nuts on a baking tray (cookie sheet) and lightly toast under the grill (broiler) for 2–3 minutes or until golden.

3 Soak the sultanas in a bowl of warm water for about 20 minutes. Drain the sultanas thoroughly.

4 Place the tomatoes, pine nuts and sultanas in a small pan and gently heat.

5 Add the anchovies and tomato purée, heating the sauce for a further 2–3 minutes or until hot.

6 Cook the pasta in a saucepan of boiling water according to the instructions on the packet or until it is cooked through, but still has 'bite'. Drain thoroughly.

7 Transfer the pasta to a serving plate and serve with the hot Sicilian sauce.

VARIATION

Add 100 g/3¹/₂ oz bacon, grilled for 5 minutes until crispy, then chopped, instead of the anchovies, if you prefer.

COOK'S TIP

If you are making fresh pasta, remember that pasta dough prefers warm conditions and responds well to handling. Do not leave to chill and do not use a marble surface for kneading.

Cannelloni

*It is easier to use dried pasta in this recipe – you can buy it ready made in tubes.
If you are using fresh pasta, you must cut out squares and roll them yourself.*

Serves 4

INGREDIENTS

20 tubes dried cannelloni (about
200 g/7 oz) or 20 square sheets of
fresh pasta (about 350 g/12 oz)
250 g/9 oz ricotta cheese
150 g/5^1/$_2$ oz frozen spinach,
defrosted

^{1}/$_2$ small red (bell) pepper, diced
2 spring onions (scallions), chopped
150 ml/5 fl oz/^{2}/$_3$ cup hot vegetable
or chicken stock

1 portion of Basil and Tomato Sauce
(see page 36)
5 g/1 oz Parmesan or pecorino
cheese, grated
salt and pepper

1 If you are using dried
cannelloni, check the packet
instructions; many varieties do not
need pre-cooking. If necessary,
pre-cook your pasta. Bring a large
saucepan of water to the boil, add
1 tablespoon of oil and cook the
pasta for 3–4 minutes – it is easier
to do this in batches.

2 In a bowl, mix together the
ricotta, spinach, (bell) pepper,
and spring onions (scallions)
and season to taste with salt
and pepper.

3 Lightly butter an ovenproof
dish, large enough to contain
all of the pasta tubes in a single
layer. Spoon the ricotta mixture
into the pasta tubes and place
them into the prepared dish. If
you are using fresh sheets of pasta,
spread the ricotta mixture along
one side of each fresh pasta square
and roll up to form a tube.

4 Mix together the stock and
Basil and Tomato Sauce (see
page 36) and pour over the
pasta tubes.

5 Sprinkle the cheese over
the cannelloni and bake in a
preheated oven, 190°C/375°F/Gas
Mark 5, for 20–25 minutes or until
the pasta is cooked through.

VARIATION

*If you would prefer a creamier
version, omit the stock and
the Basil and Tomato sauce
and replace with Béchamel Sauce.*

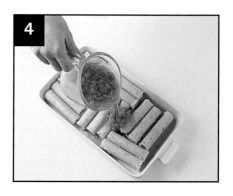

Potato Gnocchi with Tomato Sauce

Freshly made potato gnocchi are delicious, especially when they are topped with a fragrant tomato sauce.

Serves 4

INGREDIENTS

350 g/12 oz floury (mealy) potatoes (those suitable for baking or mashing), halved
75 g/2³/4 oz self-raising flour, plus extra for rolling out
2 tsp dried oregano

2 tbsp oil
1 large onion, chopped
2 garlic cloves, chopped
1 x 400g/14 oz can chopped tomatoes
¹/2 vegetable stock cube dissolved in

100ml/3¹/2 fl oz/¹/3 cup boiling water
salt and pepper
2 tbsp basil, shredded, plus whole leaves to garnish
Parmesan cheese, grated, to serve

1 Bring a large pan of water to the boil. Add the potatoes and cook for 12–15 minutes or until tender. Drain and leave to cool.

2 Peel and then mash the potatoes with the salt and pepper, sifted flour and oregano. Mix together with your hands to form a dough.

3 Heat the oil in a pan. Add the onions and garlic and cook for 3–4 minutes. Add the tomatoes and stock and cook, uncovered, for 10 minutes. Season with salt and pepper to taste.

4 Roll the potato dough into a sausage about 2.5 cm/1 inch in diameter. Cut the sausage into 2.5 cm/1 inch lengths. Flour your hands, then press a fork into each piece to create a series of ridges on one side and the indent of your index finger on the other.

5 Bring a large pan of water to the boil and cook the gnocchi, in batches, for 2–3 minutes. They should rise to the surface when cooked. Drain and keep warm.

6 Stir the basil into the tomato sauce and pour over the gnocchi. Garnish with basil leaves and freshly ground black pepper. Sprinkle with Parmesan and serve.

VARIATION

Try serving the gnocchi with Pesto Sauce for a change.

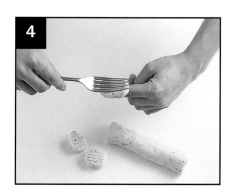

Zabaglione

This well-known dish is really a light but rich egg mousse flavoured with Marsala.

Serves 4

INGREDIENTS

5 egg yolks
100 g/3^1/$_2$ oz caster (superfine) sugar

150 ml/ 5 fl oz/^{2}/$_3$ cup Marsala or
sweet sherry

amaretti biscuits, to serve (optional)

1 Place the egg yolks in a large mixing bowl.

2 Add the caster (superfine) sugar to the egg yolks and whisk until the mixture is thick and very pale and has doubled in volume.

3 Place the bowl containing the egg yolk and sugar mixture over a saucepan of gently simmering water.

4 Add the Marsala or sherry to the egg yolk and sugar mixture and continue whisking until the foam mixture becomes warm. This process may take as long as 10 minutes.

5 Pour the mixture, which should be frothy and light, into 4 wine glasses.

6 Serve the zabaglione warm with fresh fruit or amaretti biscuits, if you wish.

VARIATION

Iced or Semifreddo Zabaglione can be made by following the method here, then continuing to whisk the foam while standing the bowl in cold water. Beat 150 ml/ ^{1}/$_4$ pint/^{2}/$_3$ cup whipping (light) cream until it just holds its shape. Fold into the foam and freeze for about 2 hours, until just frozen.

VARIATION

Any other type of liqueur may be used instead of the Marsala or sweet sherry, if you prefer. Serve soft fruits, such as strawberries or raspberries, with the zabaglione – it's a delicious combination!

Tiramisu

This is a traditional chocolate dessert from Italy, although at one time it was known as Zuppa Inglese *because it was a favourite with the English society living in Florence in the 1800's.*

Serves 6

INGREDIENTS

300 g/10¹/2 oz dark chocolate
400 g/14 oz mascarpone cheese
150 ml/5 fl oz/²/3 cup double (heavy)
   cream, whipped until it just holds
   its shape

400 ml/14 fl oz black coffee with
   50 g/1³/4 oz caster (superfine)
   sugar, cooled
6 tbsp dark rum or brandy

36 sponge fingers (lady-fingers),
   about 400 g/14 oz
cocoa powder, to dust

1 Melt the chocolate in a bowl set over a saucepan of simmering water, stirring occasionally. Leave the chocolate to cool slightly, then stir it into the mascarpone and cream.

2 Mix the coffee and rum together in a bowl. Dip the sponge fingers (lady-fingers) into the mixture briefly so that they absorb the liquid but do not become soggy.

3 Place 3 sponge fingers (lady-fingers) on 3 serving plates.

4 Spoon a layer of the mascarpone and chocolate mixture over the sponge fingers (lady-fingers).

5 Place 3 more sponge fingers (lady-fingers) on top of the mascarpone layer. Spread another layer of mascarpone and chocolate mixture and place 3 more sponge fingers (lady-fingers) on top.

6 Leave the tiramisu to chill in the refrigerator for at least 1 hour. Dust with a little cocoa powder just before serving.

COOK'S TIP

Tiramisu can also be served semi-frozen, like ice-cream. Freeze the tiramisu for 2 hours and serve immediately as it defrosts very quickly.

VARIATION

Try adding 50 g/1³/4 oz toasted, chopped hazelnuts to the chocolate cream mixture in step 1, if you prefer.

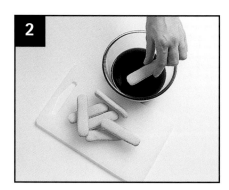

This is a Parragon Book
First published in 2003

Parragon
Queen Street House
4 Queen Street, Bath, BA1 1HE, UK

ISBN: 1-40540-825-1

Printed in China

NOTE

This book uses imperial and metric measurements. Follow the same units
of measurement throughout; do not mix imperial and metric. All spoon
measurements are level; teaspoons are assumed to be 5 ml and
tablespoons are assumed to be 15 ml. Unless otherwise stated, milk is
assumed to be whole milk, eggs and individual vegetables such as
potatoes are medium, and pepper is freshly ground black pepper.

The times given for each recipe are an approximate guide only because
the preparation times may differ according to the techniques used by
different people and the cooking times may vary as a result of the type of
oven used.

Recipes using raw or very lightly cooked eggs should be avoided by
infants, the elderly, pregnant women, convalescents and anyone suffering
from an illness.